MY DAILY GRATITUDE JOURNAL

Bring Positivity and Joy into Every Day

MY DAILY GRATITUDE JOURNAL

Compiled by Claire Plimmer and Siobhan Coleman

An Hachette UK Company
www.hachette.co.uk

Vie Books, an imprint of Summersdale Publishers Ltd
Part of Octopus Publishing Group Limited
Carmelite House
50 Victoria Embankment
LONDON
EC4Y 0DZ
UK

www.summersdale.com

Printed and bound in China

ISBN: 978-1-80007-830-7

Substantial discounts on bulk quantities of Summersdale books are available to corporations, professional associations and other organizations. For details contact general enquiries: telephone: +44 (0) 1243 771107 or email: enquiries@summersdale.com.

This journal belongs to:

_____

INTRODUCTION

It's no secret that showing gratitude is good for you – science backs this up with evidence that it can lower stress, help you sleep better and may even reduce the risk of heart disease. More and more of us are taking the time to be thankful for what we have and one of the best ways to do this is to keep a daily gratitude journal.

While regular journaling is proven to improve your well-being, making a point of jotting down all the things you're grateful for can take the experience to a whole new level. If you want to keep a gratitude journal but don't know where to start, this book has tips and prompts to help you, along with plenty of space to get creative. The great thing is that regular journaling is an easy habit to form and after a short time you will have a great collection of inspiring material. Your journal will also provide positive inspiration to look back on when you need a pick-me-up.

Gratitude journaling can be done at any time of day, but it's recommended that you do it in the morning, when you wake up, and then again in the evening. Writing a simple note about something you are grateful for can help to change your perspective and successfully set you up with a positive outlook for the day ahead. Similarly, reflecting on your day and jotting down positive statements or grateful sentiments will ensure you go to bed with a sense of contentment and joy at everything you achieved. Are you ready to begin? Your gratitude journey starts here…

Gratitude is good for you

Feeling gratitude means you are noticing the goodness in your life. By acknowledging and writing the good things down you will feel more positive, relish good experiences and build strong relationships. All in all, it's a recipe for a much happier life! Research has shown that people who write about their gratitude are more optimistic and feel better about their lives in general. In the same way that regular physical exercise improves your strength and endurance, regular gratitude journaling can boost your mental fitness.

Focusing on what you have in your life, rather than what is missing, really helps to maintain a positive outlook. Scientists have found that building feelings of contentment and satisfaction naturally counters stress and leaves you feeling much more grounded and able to deal with whatever life throws at you. This in turn eases any feelings of anxiety. The effects of gratitude journaling are not usually immediate, however. It may take a little time for the benefits to become apparent, but after several weeks you should notice a positive difference in your mental health.

Once journaling becomes a part of your daily routine, you'll be more present and mindful and, as a result, more able to appreciate the small joys each day delivers. Expressing gratitude can also have lasting effects on the brain. Studies suggest that actively acknowledging appreciation may help train the brain to be more sensitive to feeling grateful. Therefore, it is a very beneficial habit to develop. Immersing yourself in happy thoughts such as remembering an exciting event you may have experienced or recalling a romantic moment means you relive the emotions as if the occasion is happening again and this triggers endorphins – your happy hormone. A boost of happiness can help you reset your mood and find joy in your life.

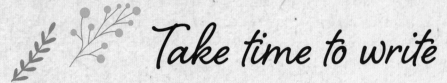

Take time to write

When you take the time to focus on the good things in your life you naturally become more positive. Writing down what you are thankful for can make you more optimistic because you are choosing to see more of the positivity in your life while giving less power to negative emotions. While these positive aspects of your life may be floating around in your subconscious, writing them down makes them more concrete and real.

To get you started, look at this positive mind map for inspiration and then use the next page to create your own positivity cloud.

Positive mind map

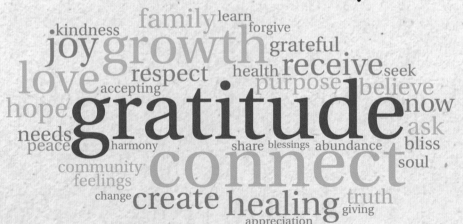

Create your own positivity cloud here by writing down everything you are grateful for...

Three good things

We are all prone to rushing about, dashing from one thing to the next without finding time to relax and focus on what is good in our lives. Creating a routine or a habit that is guaranteed to bring you joy can provide an anchor amid the busyness of life; one that helps you to feel safe, in control and connected to yourself.

When you are feeling burdened by worries, one of the best ways to lift your mood and calm yourself before bed is to think of three good things that have happened during the day. Each could be something small like receiving a compliment or having a productive meeting, but all these little occurrences will serve as a reminder that positive things happen every day.

In preparation for starting your journal habit, begin now and write down three good things that have happened to you in the last week…

Top and tail your day with gratitude

Start your day with a dose of optimism by writing down some of the things for which you feel grateful. As you go about your daily business, take time to reflect on the things that you have noted down in your journal as a reminder to keep positive. Then, at the end of your day see how many other things have cropped up for which you feel thankful.

A psychological study has shown that spending just 15 minutes before bed writing down a few grateful sentiments can help you have a much better night's sleep. By thinking of the positive experiences of the day or reminding yourself of the good things in your life, you are less likely to focus on any worries, which will help you clear your mind for a good night's sleep.

Now you know the benefits of journaling, it's over to you to start your gratitude journey.

DATE:

As I wake up today, I'm grateful for...

_____

_____

As I prepare to sleep and reflect on the day, I am grateful for...

_____

_____

DATE:

As I wake up today, I'm grateful for...

_____

_____

As I prepare to sleep and reflect on the day, I am grateful for...

_____

_____

DATE:

What are you looking forward to?

_____

_____

_____

_____

DATE:

As I wake up today, I'm grateful for...

_____

_____

_____

As I prepare to sleep and reflect on the day, I am grateful for...

_____

_____

_____

DATE:

What about your body are you grateful for?

_____

_____

_____

_____

_____

_____

_____

_____

_____

_____

DATE:

As I wake up today, I'm grateful for...

_____

_____

_____

As I prepare to sleep and reflect on the day, I am grateful for...

_____

_____

_____

Write a
thank you letter

Who would you like to say thank you to? There are likely to be many people that you are grateful for but use this space to write some notes you could include in a letter to someone thanking them for a specific action that helped you through a tough time.

_____

_____

_____

_____

_____

_____

_____

_____

_____

_____

_____

_____

_____

_____

DATE:

As I wake up today, I'm grateful for…

_____

_____

As I prepare to sleep and reflect on the day, I am grateful for…

_____

_____

DATE:

As I wake up today, I'm grateful for…

_____

_____

As I prepare to sleep and reflect on the day, I am grateful for…

_____

_____

DATE:

What do you love most about your favourite song?

_____

_____

_____

_____

_____

DATE:

As I wake up today, I'm grateful for...

_____

_____

As I prepare to sleep and reflect on the day, I am grateful for...

_____

_____

DATE:

As I wake up today, I'm grateful for...

_____

_____

As I prepare to sleep and reflect on the day, I am grateful for...

_____

_____

DATE:

Where is your happy place?

_____

_____

_____

_____

_____

_____

DATE:

As I wake up today, I'm grateful for...

_____

_____

*As I prepare to sleep and reflect on the
day, I am grateful for...*

_____

_____

DATE:

What is your favourite way to relax?

_____

_____

_____

_____

_____

_____

DATE:

As I wake up today, I'm grateful for...

_____

_____

As I prepare to sleep and reflect on the day, I am grateful for...

_____

_____

DATE:

Which people in your life are you grateful for?

_____

_____

_____

_____

DATE:

As I wake up today, I'm grateful for...

_____

_____

As I prepare to sleep and reflect on the day, I am grateful for...

_____

_____

DATE:

Which hobbies bring you joy?

_____

_____

_____

_____

DATE:

As I wake up today, I'm grateful for...

_____

_____

As I prepare to sleep and reflect on the day, I am grateful for...

_____

_____

DATE:

As I wake up today, I'm grateful for...

_____

_____

As I prepare to sleep and reflect on the day, I am grateful for...

_____

_____

DATE:

As I wake up today, I'm grateful for...

_____

_____

As I prepare to sleep and reflect on the day, I am grateful for...

_____

_____

DATE:

Think of an obstacle you have faced. How did you overcome it?

_____

_____

_____

_____

_____

DATE:

As I wake up today, I'm grateful for...

_____

_____

As I prepare to sleep and reflect on the day, I am grateful for...

_____

_____

DATE:

As I wake up today, I'm grateful for...

_____

_____

As I prepare to sleep and reflect on the day, I am grateful for...

_____

_____

DATE:

What's the best gift you have ever received?

_____

_____

_____

_____

_____

_____

_____

_____

_____

_____

DATE:

As I wake up today, I'm grateful for…

_____

_____

_____

_____

As I prepare to sleep and reflect on the day, I am grateful for…

_____

_____

_____

_____

DATE:

As I wake up today, I'm grateful for…

_____

_____

_____

_____

As I prepare to sleep and reflect on the day, I am grateful for…

_____

_____

_____

_____

DATE:

What do you love most about your favourite film?

_____

_____

_____

_____

_____

_____

_____

DATE:

Who was the last person to make you smile and what did they do?

_____

_____

_____

_____

_____

_____

_____

DATE:

As I wake up today, I'm grateful for...

_____

_____

_____

_____

As I prepare to sleep and reflect on the day, I am grateful for...

_____

_____

_____

DATE:

As I wake up today, I'm grateful for...

_____

_____

_____

_____

As I prepare to sleep and reflect on the day, I am grateful for...

_____

_____

_____

DATE:

As I wake up today, I'm grateful for...

_____

_____

_____

_____

_____

As I prepare to sleep and reflect on the day, I am grateful for...

_____

_____

_____

_____

_____

DATE:

What's the one thing that always cheers you up?

_____

_____

_____

_____

_____

_____

_____

DATE:

What do you like most about yourself?

_____

_____

_____

_____

_____

_____

_____

_____

DATE:

As I wake up today, I'm grateful for...

_____

_____

_____

_____

As I prepare to sleep and reflect on the day, I am grateful for...

_____

_____

_____

DATE:

As I wake up today, I'm grateful for...

_____

_____

_____

_____

As I prepare to sleep and reflect on the day, I am grateful for...

_____

_____

_____

Date:

As I wake up today, I'm grateful for...

_____

_____

As I prepare to sleep and reflect on the day, I am grateful for...

_____

_____

Date:

What is your favourite me time activity?

_____

_____

_____

_____

_____

_____

_____

_____

Date:

As I wake up today, I'm grateful for...

_____

_____

_____

_____

As I prepare to sleep and reflect on the day, I am grateful for...

_____

_____

_____

_____

Date:

As I wake up today, I'm grateful for...

_____

_____

_____

_____

As I prepare to sleep and reflect on the day, I am grateful for...

_____

_____

_____

_____

Date:

What was the last thing that made you laugh?

_____

_____

_____

_____

_____

_____

Write a grateful poem

It doesn't matter how cheesy it might seem — the more positive words you use the better.

_____
_____
_____
_____
_____
_____
_____
_____
_____
_____
_____
_____
_____
_____
_____
_____
_____

Date:

As I wake up today, I'm grateful for...

_____

_____

_____

_____

As I prepare to sleep and reflect on the day, I am grateful for...

_____

_____

_____

Date:

As I wake up today, I'm grateful for...

_____

_____

_____

_____

As I prepare to sleep and reflect on the day, I am grateful for...

_____

_____

_____

Date:

List five good things that have happened in the last year...

_____

_____

_____

_____

_____

_____

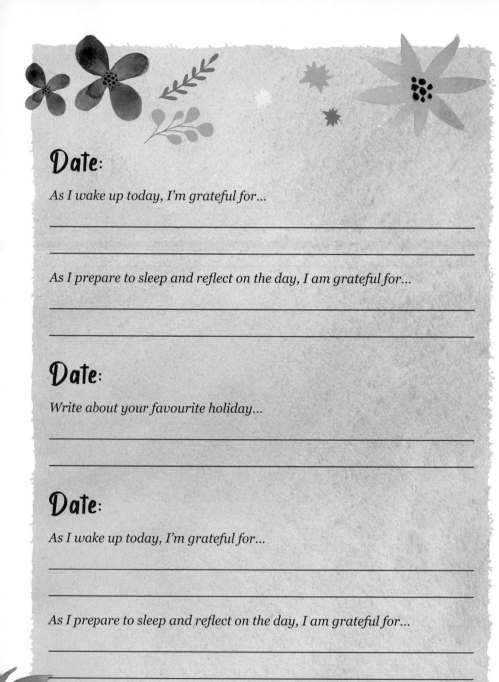

Date:

As I wake up today, I'm grateful for...

_____

_____

As I prepare to sleep and reflect on the day, I am grateful for...

_____

_____

Date:

Write about your favourite holiday...

_____

_____

Date:

As I wake up today, I'm grateful for...

_____

_____

As I prepare to sleep and reflect on the day, I am grateful for...

_____

_____

Date:

As I wake up today, I'm grateful for...

_____

_____

_____

_____

As I prepare to sleep and reflect on the day, I am grateful for...

_____

_____

_____

_____

Date:

As I wake up today, I'm grateful for...

_____

_____

_____

_____

As I prepare to sleep and reflect on the day, I am grateful for...

_____

_____

_____

_____

Date:

Describe your favourite outfit. What makes it your favourite?

_____

_____

_____

_____

_____

_____

_____

Date:

Describe an experience that was difficult. What did it teach you?

_____

_____

_____

_____

_____

_____

_____

_____

_____

_____

Date:

As I wake up today, I'm grateful for...

_____

_____

_____

As I prepare to sleep and reflect on the day, I am grateful for...

_____

_____

_____

_____

Date:

As I wake up today, I'm grateful for...

_____

_____

_____

_____

As I prepare to sleep and reflect on the day, I am grateful for...

_____

_____

_____

_____

Date:

What makes you beautiful?

_____

_____

_____

_____

_____

_____

_____

_____

_____

_____

Date:

As I wake up today, I'm grateful for...

_____

_____

As I prepare to sleep and reflect on the day, I am grateful for...

_____

_____

Date:

What's your favourite season of the year and why does it bring you joy?

_____

_____

_____

_____

_____

Date:

As I wake up today, I'm grateful for...

_____

_____

As I prepare to sleep and reflect on the day, I am grateful for...

_____

_____

Date:

What's your favourite quote and why does it inspire you?

_____

_____

_____

_____

_____

Date:

As I wake up today, I'm grateful for...

_____

_____

As I prepare to sleep and reflect on the day, I am grateful for...

_____

_____

Date:

As I wake up today, I'm grateful for...

_____

_____

As I prepare to sleep and reflect on the day, I am grateful for...

_____

_____

Date:

As I wake up today, I'm grateful for...

_____

_____

_____

_____

As I prepare to sleep and reflect on the day, I am grateful for...

_____

_____

_____

_____

Date:

When was the last time someone helped you with a problem?

_____

_____

_____

_____

_____

_____

_____

_____

Date:

What do you like best about the morning?

_____
_____
_____
_____
_____
_____

Date:

As I wake up today, I'm grateful for...

_____
_____
_____
_____
_____

As I prepare to sleep and reflect on the day, I am grateful for...

_____
_____
_____
_____
_____

DATE:

As I wake up today, I'm grateful for...

_____

_____

As I prepare to sleep and reflect on the day, I am grateful for...

_____

_____

DATE:

What do you like best about the evening?

_____

_____

_____

_____

_____

DATE:

As I wake up today, I'm grateful for...

_____

_____

As I prepare to sleep and reflect on the day, I am grateful for...

_____

_____

_____

DATE:

As I wake up today, I'm
grateful for...

_____

_____

_____

As I prepare to sleep and
reflect on the day, I am
grateful for...

_____

_____

_____

DATE:

As I wake up today, I'm
grateful for...

_____

_____

_____

As I prepare to sleep and
reflect on the day, I am
grateful for...

_____

_____

_____

DATE:

What are your favourite lyrics and why do they inspire you?

_____

_____

_____

_____

_____

_____

DATE:

What's the most courageous thing you have ever done?

_____

_____

_____

_____

_____

DATE:

As I wake up today, I'm grateful for...

_____

_____

As I prepare to sleep and reflect on the day, I am grateful for...

_____

_____

DATE:

As I wake up today, I'm grateful for...

_____

_____

As I prepare to sleep and reflect on the day,
I am grateful for...

_____

_____

DATE:

What was the last compliment you received?

_____

_____

_____

_____

_____

_____

DATE:

As I wake up today, I'm grateful for...

_____

_____

As I prepare to sleep and reflect on the day, I am grateful for...

_____

_____

DATE:

What's your favourite meal and what do you love about it?

_____

_____

_____

_____

DATE:

As I wake up today, I'm grateful for...

_____

_____

As I prepare to sleep and reflect on the day, I am grateful for...

_____

_____

Date:

As I wake up today, I'm grateful for...

_____

_____

As I prepare to sleep and reflect on the day, I am grateful for...

_____

_____

Date:

As I wake up today, I'm grateful for...

_____

_____

As I prepare to sleep and reflect on the day, I am grateful for...

_____

_____

Date:

Describe a time when you faced your fears...

_____

_____

_____

_____

_____

DATE:

Describe all the things you love most about your home...

_____

_____

_____

_____

_____

_____

DATE:

As I wake up today, I'm grateful for...

_____

_____

As I prepare to sleep and reflect on the day, I am grateful for...

_____

_____

DATE:

As I wake up today, I'm grateful for...

_____

_____

As I prepare to sleep and reflect on the day, I am grateful for...

_____

_____

DATE:

What was the best thing that happened today?

_____

_____

_____

_____

_____

DATE:

As I wake up today, I'm grateful for...

_____

_____

_____

_____

As I prepare to sleep and reflect on the day, I am grateful for...

_____

_____

_____

DATE:

As I wake up today, I'm grateful for...

_____

_____

_____

_____

As I prepare to sleep and reflect on the day, I am grateful for...

_____

_____

_____

DATE:

What have you learned recently?

_____

_____

_____

_____

_____

_____

_____

DATE:

What's the nicest thing someone has ever done for you?

_____
_____
_____
_____
_____
_____
_____

DATE:

As I wake up today, I'm grateful for...

_____
_____
_____
_____

As I prepare to sleep and reflect on the day, I am grateful for...

_____
_____
_____

DATE:

As I wake up today, I'm grateful for...

_____
_____
_____
_____

As I prepare to sleep and reflect on the day, I am grateful for...

_____
_____
_____

DATE:

As I wake up today, I'm grateful for...

_____

_____

_____

_____

As I prepare to sleep and reflect on the day, I am grateful for...

_____

_____

_____

_____

DATE:

What is your proudest achievement?

_____

_____

_____

_____

_____

_____

_____

_____

_____

DATE:

Describe a good deed you have done that really made a difference...

_____

_____

_____

_____

_____

_____

_____

DATE:

As I wake up today, I'm grateful for...

_____

_____

_____

_____

As I prepare to sleep and reflect on the day, I am grateful for...

_____

_____

_____

_____

DATE:

As I wake up today, I'm grateful for…

_____

_____

_____

_____

As I prepare to sleep and reflect on the day, I am grateful for…

_____

_____

_____

DATE:

As I wake up today, I'm grateful for…

_____

_____

_____

_____

As I prepare to sleep and reflect on the day, I am grateful for…

_____

_____

_____

DATE:

What's your favourite thing to do on a sunny day?

_____

_____

_____

_____

_____

_____

_____

DATE:

As I wake up today, I'm grateful for...

_____

_____

_____

_____

As I prepare to sleep and reflect on the day, I am grateful for...

_____

_____

_____

DATE:

As I wake up today, I'm grateful for...

_____

_____

_____

_____

As I prepare to sleep and reflect on the day, I am grateful for...

_____

_____

_____

DATE:

What's your favourite thing to do on a rainy day?

_____

_____

_____

_____

_____

_____

Acknowledge a friend

Write a list of all the kind things that you could say about your best friend. What makes that person special to you? Why are you glad that you have that friendship?

_____

_____

_____

_____

_____

_____

_____

_____

_____

_____

_____

_____

_____

_____

_____

_____

_____

Date:

What have you achieved since this time last year?

_____

_____

_____

_____

_____

_____

_____

Date:

As I wake up today, I'm grateful for...

_____

_____

_____

_____

As I prepare to sleep and reflect on the day, I am grateful for...

_____

_____

_____

_____

Date:

As I wake up today, I'm grateful for...

_____

_____

_____

_____

As I prepare to sleep and reflect on the day, I am grateful for...

_____

_____

_____

_____

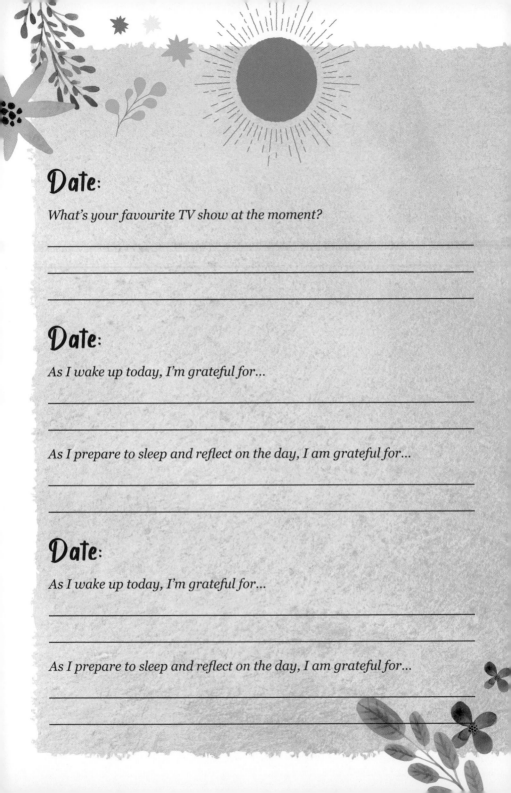

Date:

What's your favourite TV show at the moment?

_____

_____

_____

Date:

As I wake up today, I'm grateful for...

_____

_____

As I prepare to sleep and reflect on the day, I am grateful for...

_____

_____

Date:

As I wake up today, I'm grateful for...

_____

_____

As I prepare to sleep and reflect on the day, I am grateful for...

_____

_____

Date:

As I wake up today, I'm grateful for...

_____

_____

_____

_____

As I prepare to sleep and reflect on the day, I am grateful for...

_____

_____

_____

_____

Date:

As I wake up today, I'm grateful for...

_____

_____

_____

_____

As I prepare to sleep and reflect on the day, I am grateful for...

_____

_____

_____

_____

Date:

When was the last time you helped someone with a problem?

_____

_____

_____

_____

_____

_____

_____

Date:

As I wake up today, I'm grateful for...

_____

_____

_____

As I prepare to sleep and reflect on the day, I am grateful for...

_____

_____

_____

Date:

Write about someone who has made your life better...

_____

_____

_____

_____

_____

_____

_____

_____

Date:

As I wake up today, I'm grateful for...

_____

_____

_____

_____

As I prepare to sleep and reflect on the day, I am grateful for...

_____

_____

_____

_____

Date:

List the friends who make you feel great about yourself...

_____

_____

_____

_____

_____

_____

_____

Date:

As I wake up today, I'm grateful for...

_____

_____

As I prepare to sleep and reflect on the day, I am grateful for...

_____

_____

Date:

What talents do you have that you are grateful for?

_____

_____

_____

_____

_____

_____

_____

Date:

As I wake up today, I'm grateful for...

_____

_____

As I prepare to sleep and reflect on the day, I am grateful for...

_____

_____

Date:

As I wake up today, I'm grateful for...

_____

_____

*As I prepare to sleep and reflect on the
day, I am grateful for...*

_____

_____

Date:

As I wake up today, I'm grateful for...

_____

_____

As I prepare to sleep and reflect on the day, I am grateful for...

_____

_____

Date:

What is your favourite time of the day and why does it make you happy?

_____

_____

_____

_____

_____

Date:

What made you laugh out loud today?

_____

_____

_____

_____

_____

_____

_____

Date:

As I wake up today, I'm grateful for...

_____

_____

As I prepare to sleep and reflect on the day, I am grateful for...

_____

_____

Date:

As I wake up today, I'm grateful for...

_____

_____

As I prepare to sleep and reflect on the day, I am grateful for...

_____

_____

Date:

As I wake up today, I'm grateful for...

_____

_____

As I prepare to sleep and reflect on the day, I am grateful for...

_____

_____

Date:

What do you love most about your friends?

_____

_____

_____

_____

_____

_____

_____

_____

_____

_____

_____

_____

Date:

As I wake up today, I'm grateful for...

_____

_____

As I prepare to sleep and reflect on the day, I am grateful for...

_____

_____

Date:

What do you love most about your family?

_____

_____

_____

_____

_____

Date:

As I wake up today, I'm grateful for...

_____

_____

As I prepare to sleep and reflect on the day, I am grateful for...

_____

_____

Date:

Describe a time when you were pleasantly surprised by something...

_____

_____

_____

_____

_____

_____

Date:

As I wake up today, I'm grateful for...

_____

_____

As I prepare to sleep and reflect on the day, I am grateful for...

_____

_____

Date:

As I wake up today, I'm grateful for...

_____

_____

As I prepare to sleep and reflect on the day, I am grateful for...

_____

_____

DATE:

As I wake up today, I'm grateful for...

_____

_____

As I prepare to sleep and reflect on the day, I am grateful for...

_____

_____

DATE:

Think of a time when something exceeded your expectations...

_____

_____

_____

_____

_____

_____

_____

_____

_____

_____

_____

DATE:

As I wake up today, I'm grateful for...

_____

_____

_____

_____

As I prepare to sleep and reflect on the day, I am grateful for...

_____

_____

_____

_____

DATE:

What do you love most about where you live?

_____

_____

_____

_____

_____

_____

DATE:

As I wake up today, I'm grateful for...

_____

_____

As I prepare to sleep and reflect on the day,
I am grateful for...

_____

_____

DATE:

Write about a time when someone went out of
their way to help you...

_____

_____

_____

_____

DATE:

As I wake up today, I'm grateful for...

_____

_____

As I prepare to sleep and reflect on the day,
I am grateful for...

_____

_____

DATE:

As I wake up today, I'm grateful for...

_____

_____

As I prepare to sleep and reflect on the day,
I am grateful for...

_____

_____

DATE:

As I wake up today, I'm grateful for...

_____

_____

As I prepare to sleep and reflect on the day,
I am grateful for...

_____

_____

DATE:

What's your favourite pastime?

_____

_____

_____

_____

_____

DATE:

As I wake up today, I'm grateful for...

_____

_____

As I prepare to sleep and reflect on the day, I am grateful for...

_____

_____

DATE:

What do you enjoy about being outdoors?

_____

_____

_____

_____

_____

_____

_____

_____

_____

_____

_____

DATE:

What do you enjoy about being indoors?

_____

_____

_____

_____

_____

_____

_____

_____

_____

_____

DATE:

As I wake up today, I'm grateful for...

_____

_____

As I prepare to sleep and reflect on the day, I am grateful for...

_____

_____

DATE:

As I wake up today, I'm grateful for...

_____

_____

As I prepare to sleep and reflect on the day, I am grateful for...

_____

_____

DATE:

Describe a time in your life when you felt lucky...

_____

_____

_____

_____

_____

DATE:

As I wake up today, I'm grateful for...

_____

_____

As I prepare to sleep and reflect on the day, I am grateful for...

_____

_____

DATE:

As I wake up today, I'm grateful for...

_____

_____

As I prepare to sleep and reflect on the day, I am grateful for...

_____

_____

DATE:

As I wake up today, I'm grateful for...

_____

_____

As I prepare to sleep and reflect on the day, I am grateful for...

_____

_____

DATE:

What simple things in life are you grateful for?

_____

_____

_____

_____

_____

_____

Pay it forward

Use this space to write down ideas for positive giving. What are your motivations for your charitable act?

_____

_____

_____

_____

_____

_____

_____

_____

_____

_____

_____

_____

_____

_____

_____

_____

_____

_____

_____

_____

_____

_____

DATE:

*As I wake up today,
I'm grateful for...*

_____

_____

_____

_____

*As I prepare to sleep and
reflect on the day, I am
grateful for...*

_____

_____

_____

DATE:

*As I wake up today, I'm
grateful for...*

_____

_____

_____

_____

*As I prepare to sleep and
reflect on the day, I am
grateful for...*

_____

_____

_____

DATE:

What's your favourite self-care activity?

_____

_____

_____

_____

_____

_____

_____

DATE:

As I wake up today, I'm grateful for...

_____

_____

_____

_____

As I prepare to sleep and reflect on the day, I am grateful for...

_____

_____

_____

_____

DATE:

As I wake up today, I'm grateful for...

_____

_____

_____

_____

As I prepare to sleep and reflect on the day, I am grateful for...

_____

_____

_____

_____

DATE:

What do you love most about your personality?

_____

_____

_____

_____

_____

_____

_____

DATE:

As I wake up today, I'm grateful for...

_____

_____

_____

_____

As I prepare to sleep and reflect on the day, I am grateful for...

_____

_____

_____

DATE:

As I wake up today, I'm grateful for...

_____

_____

_____

_____

As I prepare to sleep and reflect on the day, I am grateful for...

_____

_____

_____

DATE:

What's your favourite book and how does it make you feel?

_____

_____

_____

_____

_____

_____

_____

DATE:

Describe one of your favourite memories...

_____

_____

_____

_____

_____

_____

_____

_____

DATE:

As I wake up today, I'm grateful for...

_____

_____

_____

_____

As I prepare to sleep and reflect on the day, I am grateful for...

_____

_____

_____

DATE:

As I wake up today, I'm grateful for...

_____

_____

_____

_____

As I prepare to sleep and reflect on the day, I am grateful for...

_____

_____

_____

DATE:

As I wake up today, I'm grateful for...

_____

_____

_____

_____

As I prepare to sleep and reflect on the day, I am grateful for...

_____

_____

_____

DATE:

As I wake up today, I'm grateful for...

_____

_____

_____

_____

As I prepare to sleep and reflect on the day, I am grateful for...

_____

_____

_____

DATE:

When was the last time you made someone smile?

_____

_____

_____

_____

_____

_____

Date:

What is your favourite possession and why are you grateful for it?

_____

_____

_____

Date:

As I wake up today, I'm grateful for...

_____

_____

As I prepare to sleep and reflect on the day, I am grateful for...

_____

_____

Date:

As I wake up today, I'm grateful for...

_____

_____

As I prepare to sleep and reflect on the day, I am grateful for...

_____

_____

Date:

As I wake up today, I'm grateful for...

_____

_____

_____

_____

As I prepare to sleep and reflect on the day, I am grateful for...

_____

_____

_____

_____

Date:

As I wake up today, I'm grateful for...

_____

_____

_____

_____

As I prepare to sleep and reflect on the day, I am grateful for...

_____

_____

_____

_____

Date:

Which person are you looking forward to seeing in the next week?

_____

_____

_____

_____

_____

_____

_____

Date:

As I wake up today, I'm grateful for...

_____

_____

As I prepare to sleep and reflect on the day, I am grateful for...

_____

_____

Date:

Think of a photo that brings back happy memories. Write about the memories here...

_____

_____

_____

_____

_____

_____

_____

_____

Date:

As I wake up today, I'm grateful for...

_____

_____

_____

_____

As I prepare to sleep and reflect on the day, I am grateful for...

_____

_____

_____

_____

Date:

What is your favourite thing to look at?

_____

_____

_____

_____

_____

_____

_____

Date:

As I wake up today, I'm grateful for...

_____

_____

As I prepare to sleep and reflect on the day, I am grateful for...

_____

_____

Date:

What's your favourite sound?

_____

_____

_____

Date:

As I wake up today, I'm grateful for...

_____

_____

As I prepare to sleep and reflect on the day, I am grateful for...

_____

_____

Date:

As I wake up today, I'm grateful for...

_____

_____

_____

As I prepare to sleep and reflect on the day, I am grateful for...

_____

_____

_____

Date:

As I wake up today, I'm grateful for...

_____

_____

_____

As I prepare to sleep and reflect on the day, I am grateful for...

_____

_____

_____

Date:

Look around the room and list three things you are grateful for...

_____

_____

_____

_____

_____

_____

Date:

What are you most looking forward to about this weekend?

_____

_____

_____

_____

_____

_____

_____

_____

_____

_____

Date:

As I wake up today, I'm grateful for...

_____

_____

_____

As I prepare to sleep and reflect on the day, I am grateful for...

_____

_____

_____

_____

Date:

As I wake up today, I'm grateful for...

_____

_____

_____

_____

As I prepare to sleep and reflect on the day, I am grateful for...

_____

_____

_____

_____

Date:

What's your favourite colour and how does it make you feel?

_____

_____

_____

_____

_____

_____

_____

_____

_____

_____

Date:

As I wake up today, I'm grateful for...

_____

_____

As I prepare to sleep and reflect on the day, I am grateful for...

_____

_____

Date:

What was the last thing you saw that you thought was truly beautiful?

_____

_____

_____

_____

_____

_____

_____

Date:

As I wake up today, I'm grateful for...

_____

_____

As I prepare to sleep and reflect on the day, I am grateful for...

_____

_____

Date:

As I wake up today, I'm grateful for...

_____

_____

As I prepare to sleep and reflect on the day, I am grateful for...

_____

_____

Date:

As I wake up today, I'm grateful for...

_____

_____

As I prepare to sleep and reflect on the day, I am grateful for...

_____

_____

Date:

Describe a time you gave someone a gift that they were delighted to receive...

_____

_____

_____

_____

_____

Date:

Describe an act of kindness that warmed your heart...

_____

_____

_____

_____

_____

_____

_____

_____

Date:

As I wake up today, I'm grateful for...

_____

_____

_____

_____

As I prepare to sleep and reflect on the day, I am grateful for...

_____

_____

_____

_____

Date:

As I wake up today, I'm grateful for...

_____

_____

As I prepare to sleep and reflect on the day, I am grateful for...

_____

_____

Date:

How do you reward yourself for a job well done?

_____

_____

_____

_____

_____

_____

_____

_____

_____

_____

_____

_____

_____

_____

_____

DATE:

As I wake up today, I'm grateful for...

_____

_____

As I prepare to sleep and reflect on the day, I am grateful for...

_____

_____

DATE:

Describe the last time you paid a compliment to someone and it made them smile...

_____

_____

_____

_____

DATE:

As I wake up today, I'm grateful for...

_____

_____

As I prepare to sleep and reflect on the day, I am grateful for...

_____

_____

DATE:

As I wake up today, I'm grateful for...

_____

_____

_____

_____

As I prepare to sleep and reflect on the day, I am grateful for...

_____

_____

_____

_____

DATE:

As I wake up today, I'm grateful for...

_____

_____

_____

_____

As I prepare to sleep and reflect on the day, I am grateful for...

_____

_____

DATE:

Describe the last time you made someone laugh...

_____

_____

_____

_____

_____

_____

DATE:

Describe a romantic moment that filled you with joy...

_____

_____

_____

_____

_____

DATE:

As I wake up today, I'm grateful for...

_____

_____

As I prepare to sleep and reflect on the day, I am grateful for...

_____

_____

DATE:

As I wake up today, I'm grateful for...

_____

_____

As I prepare to sleep and reflect on the day, I am grateful for...

_____

_____

DATE:

What do you think makes you unique?

_____

_____

_____

_____

_____

_____

DATE:

As I wake up today, I'm grateful for...

_____

_____

As I prepare to sleep and reflect on the day, I am grateful for...

_____

_____

DATE:

Write about a time in your life when you showed resilience...

_____

_____

_____

_____

DATE:

As I wake up today, I'm grateful for...

_____

_____

As I prepare to sleep and reflect on the day, I am grateful for...

_____

_____

DATE:

As I wake up today, I'm grateful for...

_____

_____

As I prepare to sleep and reflect on the day, I am grateful for...

_____

_____

DATE:

As I wake up today, I'm grateful for...

_____

_____

As I prepare to sleep and reflect on the day, I am grateful for...

_____

_____

DATE:

List the things you do to take care of yourself...

_____

_____

_____

_____

_____

DATE:

Write about a time you had a deep conversation and really connected with someone...

_____

_____

_____

_____

_____

_____

_____

_____

_____

_____

DATE:

As I wake up today, I'm grateful for...

_____

_____

As I prepare to sleep and reflect on the day, I am grateful for...

_____

_____

DATE:

As I wake up today, I'm grateful for...

_____

_____

As I prepare to sleep and reflect on the day, I am grateful for...

_____

_____

DATE:

What do you love about your best friend?

_____

_____

_____

_____

_____

_____

_____

_____

_____

_____

_____

_____

DATE:

As I wake up today, I'm grateful for...

_____
_____
_____
_____

As I prepare to sleep and reflect on the day, I am grateful for...

_____
_____
_____
_____

DATE:

As I wake up today, I'm grateful for...

_____
_____
_____
_____

As I prepare to sleep and reflect on the day, I am grateful for...

_____
_____
_____
_____

DATE:

Describe the last time you had a nice warm hug...

_____
_____
_____
_____
_____
_____
_____

DATE:

As I wake up today, I'm grateful for...

_____

_____

_____

_____

As I prepare to sleep and reflect on the day, I am grateful for...

_____

_____

_____

DATE:

As I wake up today, I'm grateful for...

_____

_____

_____

_____

As I prepare to sleep and reflect on the day, I am grateful for...

_____

_____

_____

DATE:

Describe your favourite food and why it makes you feel happy...

_____

_____

_____

_____

_____

_____

_____

DATE:

What do you love about your bed?

_____

_____

_____

_____

_____

_____

_____

_____

_____

_____

_____

_____

_____

DATE:

As I wake up today, I'm grateful for...

_____

_____

As I prepare to sleep and reflect on the day, I am grateful for...

_____

_____

DATE:

As I wake up today, I'm grateful for...

_____

_____

As I prepare to sleep and reflect on the day, I am grateful for...

_____

_____

DATE:

What part of your morning routine do you most look forward to?

_____

_____

_____

_____

_____

_____

_____

_____

_____

_____

_____

_____

DATE:

What part of your evening routine do you most look forward to?

_____
_____
_____
_____
_____
_____
_____
_____

DATE:

As I wake up today, I'm grateful for...

_____
_____
_____
_____

As I prepare to sleep and reflect on the day, I am grateful for...

_____
_____
_____

DATE:

As I wake up today, I'm grateful for...

_____
_____
_____
_____

As I prepare to sleep and reflect on the day, I am grateful for...

_____
_____
_____

DATE:

*As I wake up today, I'm
grateful for...*

_____

_____

_____

_____

*As I prepare to sleep and
reflect on the day, I am
grateful for...*

_____

_____

_____

DATE:

*As I wake up today, I'm
grateful for...*

_____

_____

_____

_____

*As I prepare to sleep and
reflect on the day, I am
grateful for...*

_____

_____

_____

DATE:

Write about a dream you've had that made you feel good...

_____

_____

_____

_____

_____

_____

_____

Date:

As I wake up today, I'm grateful for...

_____

_____

As I prepare to sleep and reflect on the day, I am grateful for...

_____

_____

Date:

Where is your favourite place to go for a walk?

_____

_____

_____

_____

_____

_____

_____

_____

_____

_____

Date:

What physical activity always boosts your mood?

_____
_____
_____
_____
_____
_____
_____

Date:

As I wake up today, I'm grateful for...

_____
_____
_____
_____

As I prepare to sleep and reflect on the day, I am grateful for...

_____
_____
_____
_____

Date:

As I wake up today, I'm grateful for...

_____

_____

As I prepare to sleep and reflect on the day, I am grateful for...

_____

_____

Date:

Describe a time you felt completely at peace...

_____

_____

_____

_____

Date:

As I wake up today, I'm grateful for...

_____

_____

As I prepare to sleep and reflect on the day, I am grateful for...

_____

_____

Date:

As I wake up today, I'm grateful for...

_____

_____

_____

As I prepare to sleep and reflect on the day, I am grateful for...

_____

_____

_____

Date:

As I wake up today, I'm grateful for...

_____

_____

_____

As I prepare to sleep and reflect on the day, I am grateful for...

_____

_____

_____

Date:

What inspires you?

_____

_____

_____

_____

_____

_____

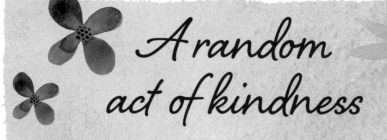

A random act of kindness

Think of a wonderful thing you could do to brighten somebody's day.
Use the space here to plot your ideas.

_____

_____

_____

_____

_____

_____

_____

_____

_____

_____

_____

_____

_____

_____

_____

_____

_____

_____

Date:

As I wake up today, I'm grateful for...

_____

_____

_____

_____

As I prepare to sleep and reflect on the day, I am grateful for...

_____

_____

_____

_____

Date:

As I wake up today, I'm grateful for...

_____

_____

_____

_____

As I prepare to sleep and reflect on the day, I am grateful for...

_____

_____

_____

_____

Date:

List the ways you can show gratitude for the amazing people in your life...

_____

_____

_____

_____

_____

_____

Date:

As I wake up today, I'm grateful for...

_____

_____

As I prepare to sleep and reflect on the day, I am grateful for...

_____

_____

Date:

What small things have happened in the last week that you're grateful for?

_____

_____

_____

_____

_____

_____

_____

Date:

As I wake up today, I'm grateful for...

_____

_____

As I prepare to sleep and reflect on the day, I am grateful for...

_____

_____

Date:

As I wake up today, I'm grateful for...

_____

_____

As I prepare to sleep and reflect on the day, I am grateful for...

_____

_____

Date:

As I wake up today, I'm grateful for...

_____

_____

As I prepare to sleep and reflect on the day, I am grateful for...

_____

_____

Date:

Which of your physical features do you like the best?

_____

_____

_____

_____

_____

Date:

List the ways you can share your gratitude with others...

_____

_____

_____

_____

_____

_____

Date:

As I wake up today, I'm grateful for...

_____

_____

As I prepare to sleep and reflect on the day, I am grateful for...

_____

_____

Date:

As I wake up today, I'm grateful for...

_____

_____

As I prepare to sleep and reflect on the day, I am grateful for...

_____

_____

Date:

As I wake up today, I'm grateful for...

_____

_____

As I prepare to sleep and reflect on the day, I am grateful for...

_____

_____

Date:

Write down a piece of positive news you heard recently...

_____

_____

_____

_____

_____

_____

_____

_____

_____

_____

_____

_____

_____

Date:

Describe a time you connected with someone new...

_____

_____

_____

_____

_____

Date:

As I wake up today, I'm grateful for...

_____

_____

As I prepare to sleep and reflect on the day, I am grateful for...

_____

_____

Date:

As I wake up today, I'm grateful for...

_____

_____

As I prepare to sleep and reflect on the day, I am grateful for...

_____

_____

Date:

As I wake up today, I'm grateful for...

_____

_____

As I prepare to sleep and reflect on the day, I am grateful for...

_____

_____

Date:

Think of something you could say to a loved one, or to yourself, to cheer them up when they're feeling down...

_____

_____

_____

_____

_____

Date:

As I wake up today, I'm grateful for...

_____

_____

As I prepare to sleep and reflect on the day, I am grateful for...

_____

_____

DATE:

As I wake up today, I'm grateful for...

_____

_____

As I prepare to sleep and reflect on the day, I am grateful for...

_____

_____

DATE:

What are your favourite smells, and do they evoke certain memories?

_____

_____

_____

_____

_____

_____

_____

_____

_____

_____

_____

_____

_____

_____

DATE:

List the people in your life
who make you feel safe and
cared for...

_____

_____

_____

_____

_____

_____

_____

_____

_____

DATE:

As I wake up today, I'm grateful for...

_____

_____

As I prepare to sleep and reflect on the day, I am grateful for...

_____

_____

_____

_____

DATE:

As I wake up today, I'm grateful for...

_____

_____

As I prepare to sleep and reflect on the day,
I am grateful for...

_____

_____

DATE:

Write about a childhood memory that fills you
with joy...

_____

_____

_____

_____

DATE:

As I wake up today, I'm grateful for...

_____

_____

As I prepare to sleep and reflect on the day, I
am grateful for...

_____

_____

DATE:

As I wake up today, I'm grateful for...

_____

_____

As I prepare to sleep and reflect on the day, I am grateful for...

_____

_____

DATE:

As I wake up today, I'm grateful for...

_____

_____

As I prepare to sleep and reflect on the day, I am grateful for...

_____

_____

DATE:

Write about the opportunities you've been given that you are grateful for...

_____

_____

_____

_____

_____

DATE:

Write about a part of your body that you're grateful for and why...

_____

_____

_____

_____

_____

DATE:

As I wake up today, I'm grateful for...

_____

_____

As I prepare to sleep and reflect on the day, I am grateful for...

_____

_____

DATE:

As I wake up today, I'm grateful for...

_____

_____

As I prepare to sleep and reflect on the day, I am grateful for...

_____

_____

DATE:

What new things do you want to learn in the next year?

_____

_____

_____

_____

_____

_____

_____

_____

_____

_____

_____

_____

DATE:

As I wake up today, I'm grateful for...

_____

_____

As I prepare to sleep and reflect on the day, I am grateful for...

_____

_____

DATE:

What would be the perfect dream you could have tonight?

_____

_____

_____

_____

DATE:

As I wake up today, I'm grateful for...

_____

_____

As I prepare to sleep and reflect on the day, I am grateful for...

_____

_____

DATE:

As I wake up today, I'm grateful for...

_____

_____

As I prepare to sleep and reflect on the day, I am grateful for...

_____

_____

DATE:

As I wake up today, I'm grateful for...

_____

_____

As I prepare to sleep and reflect on the day, I am grateful for...

_____

_____

DATE:

Describe the last YouTube video you saw that made you laugh...

_____

_____

_____

_____

DATE:

What are your favourite animals and why do they bring a smile to your face?

_____

_____

_____

_____

_____

_____

_____

_____

_____

_____

_____

_____

DATE:

As I wake up today, I'm grateful for...

_____

_____

As I prepare to sleep and reflect on the day, I am grateful for...

_____

_____

DATE:

As I wake up today, I'm grateful for...

_____

_____

_____

_____

As I prepare to sleep and reflect on the day, I am grateful for...

_____

_____

_____

_____

DATE:

What was the last delicious meal you ate that you're truly grateful for?

_____

_____

_____

_____

_____

_____

DATE:

What's your favourite TV show or film to watch when you're having a duvet day?

_____

_____

_____

_____

_____

_____

_____

DATE:

As I wake up today, I'm grateful for...

_____

_____

_____

_____

As I prepare to sleep and reflect on the day, I am grateful for...

_____

_____

_____

DATE:

As I wake up today, I'm grateful for...

_____

_____

_____

_____

As I prepare to sleep and reflect on the day, I am grateful for...

_____

_____

_____

DATE:

As I wake up today, I'm grateful for...

_____

_____

_____

_____

As I prepare to sleep and reflect on the day, I am grateful for...

_____

_____

_____

DATE:

As I wake up today, I'm grateful for...

_____

_____

_____

_____

As I prepare to sleep and reflect on the day, I am grateful for...

_____

_____

_____

DATE:

What lessons in life are you grateful to have learned?

_____

_____

_____

_____

_____

_____

_____

DATE:

As I wake up today, I'm grateful for...

_____

_____

As I prepare to sleep and reflect on the day, I am grateful for...

_____

_____

DATE:

What home comforts make you feel cosy and content?

_____

_____

_____

_____

_____

_____

_____

_____

_____

_____

_____

_____

DATE:

Which people in your life are you most grateful to have met?

_____

_____

_____

_____

_____

_____

DATE:

As I wake up today, I'm grateful for...

_____

_____

_____

_____

As I prepare to sleep and reflect on the day, I am grateful for...

_____

_____

_____

_____

Date:

As I wake up today, I'm grateful for...

_____

_____

As I prepare to sleep and reflect on the day, I am grateful for...

_____

_____

Date:

Describe a time when you overcame a setback and were left feeling stronger as a result...

_____

_____

Date:

As I wake up today, I'm grateful for...

_____

_____

As I prepare to sleep and reflect on the day, I am grateful for...

_____

_____

Date:

*As I wake up today, I'm
grateful for...*

_____

_____

_____

*As I prepare to sleep and
reflect on the day, I am
grateful for...*

_____

_____

_____

Date:

*As I wake up today, I'm
grateful for...*

_____

_____

_____

*As I prepare to sleep and
reflect on the day, I am
grateful for...*

_____

_____

_____

Date:

What makes you excited about the future?

_____

_____

_____

_____

_____

_____

_____

I am grateful for my health

Use this space to focus on your general health and note down all the things that you are most thankful for, whether it's having the clarity of mind to be able to think about this task, or being able to sleep well at night.

_____

_____

_____

_____

_____

_____

_____

_____

_____

_____

_____

_____

_____

_____

_____

_____

_____

_____

_____

Date:

As I wake up today, I'm grateful for...

_____

_____

_____

As I prepare to sleep and reflect on the day, I am grateful for...

_____

_____

_____

Date:

As I wake up today, I'm grateful for...

_____

_____

_____

As I prepare to sleep and reflect on the day, I am grateful for...

_____

_____

_____

Date:

How do you like to express yourself creatively?

_____

_____

_____

_____

_____

_____

_____

Date:

Which people in your life always make you feel at home no matter where you are?

_____

_____

_____

Date:

As I wake up today, I'm grateful for...

_____

_____

As I prepare to sleep and reflect on the day, I am grateful for...

_____

_____

Date:

As I wake up today, I'm grateful for...

_____

_____

As I prepare to sleep and reflect on the day, I am grateful for...

_____

_____

Date:

As I wake up today, I'm grateful for...

_____

_____

_____

_____

As I prepare to sleep and reflect on the day, I am grateful for...

_____

_____

_____

_____

Date:

As I wake up today, I'm grateful for...

_____

_____

_____

_____

As I prepare to sleep and reflect on the day, I am grateful for...

_____

_____

_____

_____

Date:

List three ways you can change the world for the better...

_____

_____

_____

_____

_____

_____

_____

Date:

As I wake up today, I'm grateful for...

_____

_____

As I prepare to sleep and reflect on the day, I am grateful for...

_____

_____

Date:

Write about the new places you want to visit in the next year...

_____

_____

_____

_____

_____

_____

_____

Date:

As I wake up today, I'm grateful for...

_____

_____

As I prepare to sleep and reflect on the day, I am grateful for...

_____

_____

Date:

As I wake up today, I'm grateful for...

_____

_____

As I prepare to sleep and reflect on the
day, I am grateful for...

_____

_____

Date:

Describe a time you set yourself a goal and accomplished it...

_____

_____

_____

_____

_____

_____

_____

_____

_____

_____

_____

_____

_____

Date:

What's your favourite day of the year and why?

_____

_____

_____

_____

_____

_____

Date:

As I wake up today, I'm grateful for...

_____

_____

As I prepare to sleep and reflect on the day, I am grateful for...

_____

_____

Date:

As I wake up today, I'm grateful for...

_____

_____

As I prepare to sleep and reflect on the day, I am grateful for...

_____

_____

Date:

As I wake up today, I'm grateful for...

_____

_____

As I prepare to sleep and reflect on the day, I am grateful for...

_____

_____

Date:

Describe a task you found difficult but are proud of completing...

_____

_____

_____

_____

_____

Date:

As I wake up today, I'm grateful for...

_____

_____

As I prepare to sleep and reflect on the day, I am grateful for...

_____

_____

Date:

As I wake up today, I'm grateful for...

_____

_____

As I prepare to sleep and reflect on the day, I am grateful for...

_____

_____

Date:

What's your favourite thing to do when you are by yourself?

_____

_____

_____

_____

_____

_____

_____

_____

_____

_____

_____

_____

_____

Date:

As I wake up today, I'm grateful for...

_____

_____

As I prepare to sleep and reflect on the day, I am grateful for...

_____

_____

Date:

What's your favourite thing to do when you are with others?

_____

_____

_____

_____

_____

_____

_____

_____

_____

_____

_____

_____

_____

DATE:

As I wake up today, I'm grateful for...

_____

_____

As I prepare to sleep and reflect on the day, I am grateful for...

_____

_____

_____

DATE:

List three reasons why you're grateful to live in the modern world...

_____

_____

_____

_____

_____

DATE:

As I wake up today, I'm grateful for...

_____

_____

As I prepare to sleep and reflect on the day, I am grateful for...

_____

_____

_____

DATE:

As I wake up today, I'm grateful for...

_____

_____

_____

_____

As I prepare to sleep and reflect on the day, I am grateful for...

_____

_____

_____

_____

DATE:

As I wake up today, I'm grateful for...

_____

_____

_____

As I prepare to sleep and reflect on the day, I am grateful for...

_____

_____

_____

_____

DATE:

What freedoms are you grateful to have?

_____

_____

_____

_____

_____

_____

DATE:

List the people in your life who support you and encourage you to follow your dreams...

_____

_____

_____

_____

_____

DATE:

As I wake up today, I'm grateful for...

_____

_____

As I prepare to sleep and reflect on the day, I am grateful for...

_____

_____

DATE:

As I wake up today, I'm grateful for...

_____

_____

As I prepare to sleep and reflect on the day,
I am grateful for...

_____

_____

DATE:

Describe what your perfect day would look like...

_____

_____

_____

_____

DATE:

Which single piece of advice do you think has helped shape the person you've become?

_____

_____

_____

_____

DATE:

As I wake up today, I'm grateful for...

_____

_____

As I prepare to sleep and reflect on the day, I am grateful for...

_____

_____

DATE:

As I wake up today, I'm grateful for...

_____

_____

As I prepare to sleep and reflect on the day, I am grateful for...

_____

_____

DATE:

As I wake up today, I'm grateful for...

_____

_____

As I prepare to sleep and reflect on the day, I am grateful for...

_____

_____

DATE:

Which one thing are you grateful for in your community?

_____

_____

_____

_____

_____

DATE:

As I wake up today, I'm grateful for...

_____

_____

As I prepare to sleep and reflect on the day, I am grateful for...

_____

_____

There's no place like home

Focus on your personal space. What are you thankful for? It could be that you can find peace in this haven while it could also be a place to invite friends and have fun. Use this space to jot down your thoughts.

_____

_____

_____

_____

_____

_____

_____

_____

_____

_____

_____

_____

_____

_____

_____

_____

_____

DATE:

*As I wake up today, I'm
grateful for...*

_____

_____

_____

_____

*As I prepare to sleep and
reflect on the day, I am
grateful for...*

_____

_____

_____

DATE:

*As I wake up today, I'm
grateful for...*

_____

_____

_____

_____

*As I prepare to sleep and
reflect on the day, I am
grateful for...*

_____

_____

_____

DATE:

Name one thing about today's weather that you are grateful for...

_____

_____

_____

_____

_____

_____

_____

DATE:

As I wake up today, I'm grateful for...

_____

_____

As I prepare to sleep and reflect on the day, I am grateful for...

_____

_____

DATE:

What's your favourite thing about spring?

_____

_____

_____

_____

_____

_____

_____

_____

_____

_____

_____

_____

DATE:

As I wake up today, I'm grateful for...

_____

_____

_____

_____

As I prepare to sleep and reflect on the day, I am grateful for...

_____

_____

_____

_____

DATE:

As I wake up today, I'm grateful for...

_____

_____

_____

_____

As I prepare to sleep and reflect on the day, I am grateful for...

_____

_____

_____

_____

DATE:

Write about the last time you put off a task that wasn't as bad as you thought it would be...

_____

_____

_____

_____

_____

_____

DATE:

As I wake up today, I'm grateful for...

_____

_____

_____

_____

As I prepare to sleep and reflect on the day, I am grateful for...

_____

_____

_____

_____

DATE:

As I wake up today, I'm grateful for...

_____

_____

_____

_____

As I prepare to sleep and reflect on the day, I am grateful for...

_____

_____

_____

_____

DATE:

What's your favourite thing about summer?

_____

_____

_____

_____

_____

_____

_____

DATE:

As I wake up today, I'm grateful for...

_____

_____

_____

_____

As I prepare to sleep and reflect on the day, I am grateful for...

_____

_____

_____

_____

DATE:

As I wake up today, I'm grateful for...

_____

_____

_____

_____

As I prepare to sleep and reflect on the day, I am grateful for...

_____

_____

_____

_____

DATE:

Describe a recent problem you have managed to overcome...

_____

_____

_____

_____

_____

_____

_____

DATE:

As I wake up today, I'm grateful for...

_____

_____

As I prepare to sleep and reflect on the day, I am grateful for...

_____

_____

DATE:

What's your favourite thing about autumn?

_____

_____

_____

_____

_____

_____

_____

_____

_____

_____

_____

_____

DATE:

As I wake up today, I'm grateful for...

_____

_____

As I prepare to sleep and reflect on the day, I am grateful for...

_____

_____

DATE:

What's your favourite word and how does it make you feel?

_____

_____

_____

_____

_____

_____

_____

_____

_____

_____

_____

Date:

What's your favourite thing about winter?

_____

_____

_____

Date:

As I wake up today, I'm grateful for...

_____

_____

As I prepare to sleep and reflect on the day, I am grateful for...

_____

_____

Date:

As I wake up today, I'm grateful for...

_____

_____

As I prepare to sleep and reflect on the day, I am grateful for...

_____

_____

Date:

As I wake up today, I'm
grateful for...

_____

_____

_____

_____

As I prepare to sleep and
reflect on the day, I am
grateful for...

_____

_____

_____

_____

Date:

As I wake up today, I'm
grateful for...

_____

_____

_____

_____

As I prepare to sleep and
reflect on the day, I am
grateful for...

_____

_____

_____

_____

Date:

Write about a skill you have that most people don't possess...

_____

_____

_____

_____

_____

_____

_____

FINAL WORD

Hopefully you have found gratitude journaling to be a wholly positive and fulfilling experience. The notes you have made in this very personal space will serve as a reminder for all that you have been grateful for in the space of a full year. The pages you have completed are yours to keep and reflect upon as time passes and to find joy in re-reading. Remember, there is always something to be thankful for, no matter how small, and that something can truly lift your spirits.

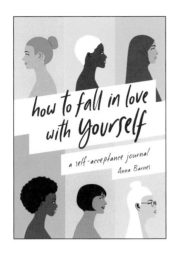

How to Fall in Love With Yourself

A Self-Acceptance Journal

Anna Barnes

978-1-78783-934-2

Paperback

Let's celebrate YOU

It's time to show yourself some love because, you know what, you are going to be spending your entire life as you.

Sometimes we lose sight of who we are and who we want to be, and what makes us special. This beautifully illustrated journal will help you to recognize and achieve your true potential. By engaging with these specially crafted tips and fill-in activities you'll find the confidence to pursue your dreams and love the skin you're in.

Take time to be kind, embrace your uniqueness and fall totally in love with yourself!

Have you enjoyed this book?
If so, why not write a review on your favourite website?

If you're interested in finding out more about our books,
find us on Facebook at Summersdale Publishers,
on Twitter at @Summersdale and on Instagram
at @summersdalebooks and get in touch.
We'd love to hear from you!

Thanks very much for buying this Summersdale book.

www.summersdale.com